Can I Rest
AWHILE?

Can I Rest AWHILE?

HEIDI LEWIS

CAN I REST AWHILE?

Published by Purposely Created Publishing Group™

Copyright © 2017 Heidi Lewis

All rights reserved.

No part of this book may be reproduced, distributed or transmitted in any form by any means, graphics, electronics, or mechanical, including photocopy, recording, taping, or by any information storage or retrieval system, without permission in writing from the publisher, except in the case of reprints in the context of reviews, quotes, or references.

Printed in the United States of America

ISBN: 978-1-947054-12-7

Special discounts are available on bulk quantity purchases by book clubs, associations and special interest groups. For details email: sales@publishyourgift.com
or call (888) 949-6228.

For information logon to: www.PublishYourGift.com

DEDICATION

For Grandma Auntie's Babies

(Jaylen & Michael)

TABLE OF CONTENTS

Acknowledgments xi
Foreword xiii
Introduction.. 1
Can I Rest Awhile? 3
This Thing Called Love 5
    Should'a Listened 6
    Dear Lord.. 7
    Dear Lord.. 8
    Dear Lord.. 9
    Dear Lord.. 10
    Dear Lord.. 11
    Dear Lord.. 12
    Dear Lord.. 13
    Coming Into Womanhood.. 14
    Thinking of You 15
    Love & Hate 17
    The Other Woman.. 18
    Daylight Come.. 19
    Collide... 20
    Men Cry In the Dark 22
    I Loved You Openly 23
    This Thing Called Love 24
    Smokey Blues Dancing.. 26

Life and Some Other Stuff 27
- On Broken Pieces.. 28
- That's What They Said.. 29
- Dreaming... 30
- Don't Worry Ma.. 31
- Little Girl... 32
- Peace 33
- Preacher Woman 34
- My Son... 35
- New York, New York 36
- Big Blue.. 37
- Walking Above 39

The Struggle is Real 41
- Cushite Nation, Arise 42
- Miss Edith 43
- Untitled 44
- Nana's Hands 45
- Trinidad 46
- Onyx... 47
- White Horse 48
- The Hood Does What the Hood Does......................... 49
- Freedom Come.. 51
- Your Black Ain't Like Mine... 52
- Daughters of Zion 53

Wonderful ME! 55
    Variations 56
    Mommy 58
    Created Anew 59
    In My Father's House 60
    I Feel Here 61
    Do You See Me? 62
    Unique 63
    Wonderful ME 65
    Breathe Again! 66
Bibliography 67
About the Author 69

ACKNOWLEDGMENTS

Lord, how can I thank you? You are my Sustainer and Victor. I love you more every day.

Mom: As a child, you were the one who wiped my tears, bandaged my scrapes, and sat by my bedside and took my vitals when I was ill. You told me I could be and do anything I wanted. Today, I know the woman you are. I understand your dreams, your fears, and even your flaws. I look back and see all the sacrifices you made. Mom, I owe you everything!

Jamie: You are the first man I ever loved. You were my friend, my ride-or-die. It wasn't until you transitioned that I realized that I needed you more than I knew. You are the inspiration for "Men Cry in the Dark." Thank you for loving me with a pure heart.

P: Thank you for listening to my stories late at night when I couldn't sleep. Your wisdom is invaluable and we both know that the Bible says, "Wisdom is the principle thing." May Ruby live on in your heart.

Shi: We are two sides of the same coin. Thank you for pushing me when fear got the better of me. I see you.

Michael and Daye: I didn't know it was possible to love anyone as much as I do you two. Your strength inspires me. Live your dreams, babies!

Punk'in: You came just when we needed you most. Because of you, I'm Auntie Lala!

Shaniqua: Your dad would be so proud of you. I love you.

Pentimenti Women Writers Group: My sisters, my tribe. We have cried and written and written and cried. Carol D, thank you for holding my hand as I wrote the title work to this project. I love each and every one of you!

Bishop and Lady Bragg: Thank you for loving me.

Finally, Bishop Sylvia Britton: You pushed me to accomplish this. Thank you.

FOREWORD

For nearly ten years, we have been blessed to serve as facilitators of the Pentimenti Women Writers Group in Dorchester, Massachusetts, a group of women who use writing as a tool to discover more about themselves, their lives, and the world around them. Some write poetry, novels, and stories, while others write family memoirs and essays. They all seek to find their voices and tell their stories, all the while committing to help each other in the process.

When we were just starting out, we did an exercise to help the women see themselves as serious writers. We went around the room and asked each woman in turn to say out loud, "I *am* a writer." For many, this was challenging; it was difficult for them to take themselves seriously and to believe—truly believe—what had previously been buried and unacknowledged dreams.

Heidi Ivey, however, was different. From the start, she seemed to *know* that she was a writer and, from the moment she joined our group and started sharing her work with us, we knew that she was a writer as well. We could feel her passion, drive, and creativity in her words, and we knew that it was only a matter of time before others felt her power.

Our only question was which of her many writings would be published first. Would it be the brilliant and heart-wrenching series of interlocking short stories about a young girl's quest to discover love and her identity? Would it be the collection of prayers and poems linked to scriptural passages in calendar form, so that they offer spiritual sustenance to readers throughout the year? Or would it be the powerful and vivid poems depicting a woman's sufferings and triumphs in the world of family and love, drugs and violence, hope and sorrow?

Further complicating Heidi's choices as a writer were the additional demands on her time and energy; after all, she is an MBA student, a minister, a business professional, an activist, and a family member and friend. How she manages to do so much and so well, we do not know. Still, in our meetings, Heidi was unfailingly present and committed, giving and engaged, as I am sure she is in all her endeavors—her writing, work, graduate studies, relationships, and ministry.

The culmination of all that work is this stunning collection of poems: *Can I Rest Awhile?* Looking over these poems, we are impressed once again by the versatility and range of Heidi's voice and the generosity and grace of her vision. Some works she wrote in our group seemed to arrive unexpectedly: At the end of a meeting, she would read a poem that had come to her that very morning, and it would be fully formed and complete. Some such as "This Thing Called Love" and "Smokey Blues Dancing" draw on the cadences and imagery of popular soul and blues music. Others such as the title poem, "Can I Rest Awhile?," are deeply rooted in the enduring tradition of African-American spirituals and hymns. And some like "Miss Edith" and "Nana's Hands" depict the people in Heidi's life, such as an elegant and formidable elderly member of our writing group and Heidi's beloved grandmother, respectively.

Heidi's poems regard the world with a gaze that is both fearless and loving. Her poems bring us into the heart of the struggles between men and women, the harrowing damage inflicted by violence and drugs, and the sustenance and grace of faith. "Should'a Listened," for example, captures almost too vividly the emotional and physical isolation of domestic violence, while "Love and Hate" conveys both the sorrows of a woman whose man is losing hope and the shame of a man who is failing his woman. Battering, drugs, and infidelity: Heidi's poems leave no stone unturned, all with grace and empathy. Still, beneath all of the suffering these poems render, hope endures, faith always awaits, and courage and resilience offer a path to redemption and wisdom.

As a person and a poet, Heidi demonstrates, above all else, generosity and kindness. You may find some of these poems painful to read; you will surely find others moving or funny, exhilarating or inspiring. They convey the full, rich, and flawed humanity of people trying for something better. Reading them will restore your spirit and help you see more clearly and love more deeply.

Laura Santel
Ann Murphy
Cambridge, Massachusetts
March 19, 2017

INTRODUCTION

As a child, I could never find the words to express how I felt. For as long as I could remember, pen and paper were my vehicle. I could be free to use my imagination and just write words I had to look up in the dictionary. Pen and paper were my hiding place. No one could take it from me or intrude. This was my world. Pen and paper drowned out the sounds of my abusive father and allowed me to close my eyes to the results of his ugliness. Pen and paper kept a fifteen-year-old from running away from home. Years later, they would keep me from losing my mind as I endured my own abusive marriage. I could cry and sob without judgment. They gave rest to a little girl and, yes, a grown woman, too afraid to sleep at night. I've been kept safe with pen and paper.

Can I Rest Awhile? bares my soul vulnerably. I have to be honest—that's a little scary. But through this work, I've found healing and forgiveness. I found my voice. My prayer is that, as you read along, you will allow healing to flood your heart and embrace the sound of your own voice.

CAN I REST AWHILE?

It's been a long hard road. I'm tired now. Can I stop and rest a while?

My feet hurt. Been running into memories. Seeing things I thought I'd forgotten.

Meeting people long dead, and unable to tell their side of the story.

It's been a long hard road. I'm weary now. Can I stop and rest awhile? My back hurts.

Been standing erect too long. Taking blow after blow.

My knees buckled a few times, but somehow I was able to stand erect again.

Been a long, hard journey. Can I close my eyes for a moment?

Need to rest awhile. Shut out the voice in my mind, reminding me of my past.

Can I breath awhile? Just take short breaths. Nothing much, just so I know I'm still alive.

Need to feel the air fill my lungs and see my chest rise and fall.

It's been a long time coming. Way too long. I'm tired now. Can I stop and rest a while?

Can I take a moment to smell the Juniper and the lily of the valley?

Reminded of better times. Times when laughter was easy and love flowed freely.

It's been a road few travel. Hard and lonely. I'm tired now, God! Can I stop and rest awhile? Ain't got much left. What I didn't give was taken from me. Oh no, not complaining.

It's a fact. Woke up one day and didn't know who I was.

I'm worn now from the fight. But can't seem to put my fist down, cause all I know is fight. Tired of the fight. Can I rest awhile? Need to massage my heart so it don't turn to stone.

Need to have a place for God to dwell. I'm exhausted now.

Can I stop and kneel in prayer for a while?

I read once in the Bible that His burden is easy and His yoke is light.

Sure don't understand all that. But here I am God. Can I stop and rest a while?

THIS THING CALLED LOVE

"Love is patient and kind. Love is not jealous or boastful or proud or rude. It does not demand its own way. It is not irritable, and it keeps no record of being wronged. It does not rejoice about injustice but rejoices whenever the truth wins out. Love never gives up, never loses faith, is always hopeful, and endures through every circumstance."

—1 Corinthians 13:4-7 (NLT)

SHOULD'A LISTENED

My daddy didn't give me to you. He wasn't there no way.

I made that choice all on my own. Made it out of loneliness and fear.

Mama kept asking, Are you sure? I was grown now. Thought I knew better than she.

Yeah, I'm sure!

Woke up the next morning with a start. Sat straight up in bed, looked around.

What have I done?

Bible says I can't divorce. Couldn't talk to Mama. She wasn't there anymore.

Believed a lie and left me when I needed her most.

Should'a listened when she tried to tell me to live my dreams.

The beatins were worse than the ones I saw my daddy give Mama. Her scars healed. But mine, well, I hid them. Brokenness can't be seen. Nobody knew how shattered I was.

Should'a listened when Mama told me I could be anything I wanted to.

But she ain't here now. I need her most. Took sides, but not mine.

Suppose I should'a listened. Thought I was grown. Thought I knew better than she.

DEAR LORD...

He got locked up today for driving without a license. I really don't want to go and bail him out.

It seems like things just go from one thing to another. I don't even know if I love the man. I don't know if I still want to be married to him.

Lord, I know I can't divorce him. And I know if he divorces me, then I can't marry again until he dies.

Lord, I don't want to be alone the rest of my life.
I need a companion.

There's nothing left between me and him.

There's no trust, we don't speak

I don't know if I believe him when he says he loves me

Lord, if I've done anything to cause this, bring it to my remembrance so I can make it right

With all my heart.

DEAR LORD...

I feel so much resentment and anger towards him. Sometimes, I think he forgets he's married.

Today, he promised to be home to heat my dinner. But, he wasn't there. It really seems like everything and everybody are more important to him than I am.

I'm so lonely

I need him here

He says he wants to try and work things out.

But it doesn't seem that way to me.

Lord, is he the man You have chosen for me?

I know I have said things and done things that weren't right.

Maybe I have no right to ask any questions of You at all.

But, Lord... I need to know

With all my heart.

DEAR LORD...

Here I kneel tonight
Needing so very much from You
Not even sure where to begin.
With all my heart.

DEAR LORD...

Another night alone.

DEAR LORD...

Thank You for Your mercy.

Thank You for the word that You gave to me to share with my brother.

Lord, I receive the word You gave to me: "Go into all the world and preach the Gospel"

Mark 16:5

Lord, I have need to be purified.

DEAR LORD...

Thank You, Father, for Your providential care over the last couple of days.

DEAR LORD....

Praise and Glory to Your name

Thank You, Father God, for delivering me.

Thank You, Lord God, for the word.

Thank You, Lord, for causing me to know

"With men this is impossible, but with God all things are possible."

Thank You, Lord.

COMING INTO WOMANHOOD

Tonight I lay with you

I endured the pain, as I gave myself to you.

I endured the sweet agony

And you took me ever so gently.

Then we held each other

Bonded as one

Slowly

I began to doze.

Behind my eyelids

I relived

My coming into Womanhood.

THINKING OF YOU

I lie awake in the darkness of the room
Watching the moon shatter its light
casting a shadow against the wall
I think of you.
I hear your voice calling my name.
I reach for you, but you're not there.
Loves gotten away from me again.
My thoughts turn to the whimsical romance we once shared,
The way you brushed your hand across my cheek
Or ran your finger down the bridge of my nose like a skillful artist tracing
His masterpiece.
How I long for you.
The cadence of your footsteps,
The smell of your cologne still lingers in the air.
In the darkness as the moon shatters its light,
I think of you.
I close my eyes and think of you.
I can still see the sideways glances from across a crowded room,
Letting me know I belong to you.
So many things spoken and unspoken,
Felt and not felt,

I think of you, in the darkness of the room.

I wonder if you're happy,

Has love found you again?

A tear slips down my cheek

In the darkness of the room.

The moon shatters its light

I long for you.

LOVE & HATE

God knows I loved you.

I believed in you

When you said you'd marry me and make a good life for yourself,

When you came home, every evening disappointed,

Watching you go out the next morning and come home the same as the night before,

I loved you.

When you started loosing hope and

began to give up

I watched you fade away from me.

You turned to alcohol and then drugs.

And then…then…

You committed a crime against God.

God knows that I hate you!

Because

You destroyed you,

And if you destroyed you

Why do I feel so damned guilty?

(Dedicated to my Aunt Hank)

THE OTHER WOMAN

I lie awake this night

Just as I have lied awake many nights before

Knowing tomorrow you will be gone.

But

Every time you come to me with the world about your shoulders

I've taken you into my arms.

I know you don't love me.

Nor do I care.

As long as I know, I love you

And maybe, one day you'll come to love me.

I know that you are a married man who is deeply in love with his wife.

I also know that when we make love or

When I think we're making love, you are only having sex.

So here I lie

While you sleep

Watching both you and the sun stir. I know in an hour you'll be gone.

And once again

I'll stand at the door with my tearful goodbyes.

You'll wipe my tears and kiss my melancholy lips

Then you'll leave.

I'll stand there until you disappear into the elevator.

DAYLIGHT COME

I may be dumb, but not stupid.

Sure, I chased you around.

I knew about you and the other women

One prettier than the other, and all prettier than me.

I heard the rumors you spread

Yeah!

I loved you (*I think*)

But Daylight Come

(*and me gone*)

COLLIDE

Our worlds collided. I am not the same. Smokey hues like a hot summer morning are my need for you. I pant at the thought of you. Trying to catch my breath. I'm in a daze.

Sweat sliding down my face pools at the base of my throat. I sigh.

Caught in a vortex of need and desire. A collision took place and I'm blown up inside. The sound of my heart thumping wildly inside my chest is more than I can stand.

Panting, I'm sure I'm going to pass out.

The memory of your scent steals my attention.

Like butterfly kisses it sweeps across my face! I crane my neck and breathe in all of you. Determined not to forget the sound of your laughter or that funny thing that you do.

The tenderness of your touch and the way you make me feel when you say "I love you."

Our worlds collided. Mine with yours, you with me.

Your imprint on my heart. I am never the same. Gone too soon I'm left behind.

Left behind to ponder should'a could'a, wanted to and didn't know how.

All things said and unsaid. Glances and reaching for you in secret.

Our worlds collided. The sound left me swaying.

A tune playing in my mind that only my heart can sing.

A stringed concerto, it rises and crescendos.

Our worlds collided and the chill of loneliness has set in.

You slipped away unaware. I'm left to wonder.

Different time, different place, no other encounter has rearranged my life

like my once in a lifetime.

Expectations, revisiting

closing my eyes seeing you,

loving you wanting you screaming for you.

My world collided.

MEN CRY IN THE DARK

God knows I loved you.

I believed in you.

When you said you'd marry me and make a good life for yourself.

When you came home every evening disappointed,

I heard your silent sobs. I saw the tears run down your face when you thought I wasn't looking.

Men Cry In the Dark

I watched you go out the next morning and come home the same as the night before.

I loved you when you started losing hope.

I watched first your eyes and then your mind become distant,

I held you in the dark and felt you shudder.

Men Cry In the Dark

I felt your spirit explode inside of you.

The silence was deafening.

I loved you when you turned to drugs to numb the pain.

Men Cry In the Dark

And then...

And then.... you committed a crime against God.

God knows, I hated you.

You destroyed you because you cried in the dark not allowing the light of the Father to fill your soul.

Men Cry In the Dark

I LOVED YOU OPENLY

God! He was black

Skin that looked like ebony

A voice that sounded like velvet. Hearing him made my world just fine.

I loved you openly.

Oh, and the smell of him changed the color prisms of my heart.

I saw myself through you. I saw me beautiful and free.

Laughter like a bell sounding in the dawn—
I loved you openly!

I saw me through you strong.

I could do anything, I could be

Anything because I loved you openly.

I gave you all of me.

I opened the secret places of me and invited you in.

You saw my brokenness, you were my healer,
my joy and my pain.

I hung on your every word, the sun rose and set in you

I loved you openly.

THIS THING CALLED LOVE

What is this thing called love?

Is it the best thing that ever happens like Gladys Knight and Pips say.

Or is it like a cool breeze that brushes across your face?

Perhaps love is that thing that causes you not to be too proud to beg

or is loving you easy because you're beautiful?

What is this thing called love?

Is it the color of amethyst or black diamonds and pearls?

Does it taste like sweet chocolate and cream?

It is a love jones? Is it the feel of your hand on the small of my back?

Or like the sound of your voice. Is it like when I argue just to hear you speak?

Is it the sweetest thing I've known? Perhaps it's that thing that Stephanie sang about?

Sweet Sensation or is it Fire and Desire? Is it Ooo la la la?

Is it simply giving you something you can feel?

What is this thing called love?

Is it like a black butterfly, soaring across the waters?

Is it the thing that causes life to have direction now and a clear point of view?

Is it that thing makes it easy because you love me, baby?

What is this thing called love? Is it a secret rendezvous?

It showed up during a time when nobody was supposed to be here.

I tried that love thang, for the last time I said. So here it is.

What is this thing called love? How did it get here?

Am I trapped by this thing called love?

SMOKEY BLUES DANCING

Lady sings the blues. Your blues, my blues, singing and crooning

Loud, in harmony as the trumpet squeals and pierces my heart.

Telling my story like she'd been there the whole time.

Smokey room filled with melancholy blues.

My life squealed out from the sound of the trumpet, pierced my heart like it knew every beat.

Lady sings the blues in hues of navy, turquoise and aqua.

Good morning, heartache, Lover man…

I shift in my seat as sweat drips between my breasts.

Too many memories, too many unwanted touches,

Eyes burning from the smoke, not sure if they're tears.

The trumpet stopped squealing but the bass played on

Doom, doom, doom, his fingers sliding up and down the strings

in the syncopated rhythm of my heart.

Blues-singing lady, telling my business to folks I ain't ever seen before.

I sit up straight in my chair, pretending she ain't singing about me.

I look around because, I feel like everyone knows.

I close my eyes and tap my foot to the sound of the scratching on the cymbals.

Play on, play on I think.

LIFE AND SOME OTHER STUFF

"For I know the thoughts that I think toward you, saith the Lord, thoughts of peace, and not of evil, to give you an expected end."

—Jeremiah 29:11 (NLT)

ON BROKEN PIECES

I looked and noticed all around me in ruins.
I realized, that it was God who brought me over!
Through all of my hurts and faults and failures
It was God who brought me over.
On Broken Pieces I have come.
I have walked through despair and hard times.
I have known great loss, great sorrow and great joy.
But...
Through it all God has promised that great
power is born from great pain.
It was on Broken Pieces that I have come.
It was only God who could give peace
when my soul was disquieted.
It was only God who caused me to live and
make it through on broken pieces.
He caused me to remain and abide in
Him when all around me was in ruin.
I realized that it was God who brought me over.
I made it on Broken Pieces!

THAT'S WHAT THEY SAID

Ugly is what they said.
I could hear their whispers and their snickering.
Clarence, the cross-eyed lion is what they said.
I could hear their whispers and their snickering.
I cast my eyes down, hoping they wouldn't see me.
Didn't they know? Didn't they care?
Their words damaged my soul.
I know how to be different. I can wear a mask.
Daddy said, Never let em' see you sweat.
That's what he said
So, I wore my mask
No one saw the crack.
No one saw the tears that slipped down my cheek.
Ugly is what they said.
Didn't they know their words damaged my soul?

DREAMING

My back is against the wall. I have nowhere turn

slowly

I'm slipping

down

down

down

Down into a black hole

Fighting, struggling

Trying to climb out

but

I'm slipping

falling

Someone, anyone

help me.

I'm drowning in the swirling sea of darkness

I can't hold on much longer

I'm begging, pleading

Drowning

I jump awake

Shaking, sweating

Am I dreaming

or is this reality?

DON'T WORRY MA

I watched as they carried me out
I watched myself float high above myself
I watched them pull the sheet over my face
I followed them down the long white hall
I heard them tell my mother
I was gone
I saw my mother's face
I saw her pain
I watched her age ten years in two minutes
I tried to reassure her
I watched the door at the end of the hall open
I saw the blinding light. I answered their call
I walked toward the light
I heard the door slam
Where I remained
For the rest of my life

LITTLE GIRL

Little girl swinging on a swing
Ribbons flying—push me higher.
Deserted and all alone,
Little girl on a swing
Ribbons flying—push me higher.
Push me higher let me touch the sky—push me higher—Ribbons flying!
Push me higher until I'm free,
Push me higher until I can spread my wings and soar.
Little girl swinging on a swing,
Deserted and all alone—Ribbons flying push me higher!

PEACE

Peace, that quiet place on the inside of me.

The place where no other voice is heard.

Peace, the sound of a babbling brook.

Peace, like the sound of the wind in fall.

Leaves swirling in the breeze and gently falling to the ground.

Peace. Like the quiet in my soul. Peace that attendeth

my way.

Peace.

A place called fullness of joy.

Peace.

A calm assurance.

Peace.

That quiet place inside.

The place where no other voice is heard.

PREACHER WOMAN

Preach'in. Too young to be preach'in. Storming down the dawn.

Caught between two worlds. Young and desirable, yet untouchable.

Wanting, but belonging to one who is Omnipresent.

Preacher woman, wanting to belong, but needing to be separate.

Preach'in down the dawn. Preach'in hard,

Wondering where she belongs—where is her place?

Preach'in hard, preach'in down the dawn,

Called to nations, but wanting to be held.

Preacher woman, torn between two worlds,

Misunderstood

Misrepresented

Miss-everything!!

Preacher woman. Preach'in hard. Storming down the dawn.

MY SON

I breathe in and out, in and out, in and out.

Birthed out of my loins, you are my greatest accomplishment.

From the moment I knew you were growing inside of me,

I breathed in and out, in and out for you.

Under my heart, I could feel your movements your dependency upon me

And mine on you, rather my need for you.

I breathe in and out, in and out, in and out for you.

Our breaths are in unison, simpatico, the perfect symphony

Like a violin concerto

You are mine and I am yours

Us, always, me and you

In and out, in and out, in and out for you.

(For P.)

NEW YORK, NEW YORK

New York, New York, the Big Apple.
New York, New York, the Big Apple.
Live and Die in Bed-Stuy! Summers in Brooklyn.
434 Jefferson Avenue between Troop and Sumpter,
Rent Parties, Fried Fish, Blue lights in the basement,
sensuous moves to congas and drums.
Fried dough, powdered sugar, 25 cents a day,
Rakim, the 5 percenter, the revolution will be televised.
Live and die in Bed-Stuy. Hot summers in Brooklyn.
Free lunches in the mini-park, offering the whole block out.
Take the shame out on me!
Ain't too proud to beg, black panthers, dashikis, fros.
New York, New York, the Big Apple.
Live and Die in Bed-Stuy. Oh, those hot summers in Brooklyn.

BIG BLUE

The Big Blue bitch as my mother called her.

Seems like everyone in my family lived there.

She was the place where all the children were born.

Hundreds of people in the backyard on the 4th of July.

Oh, the house parties. The parties, the parties, the parties.

Homemade apple pie made with apples picked from the orchard across the street.

The smells of Nana's bread and cheesecake.

I wonder what she would say if her walls could talk?

Would she say that we lived and loved as a family?

Would she say she saw more joy than pain?

Big Blue, the big blue bitch as my mother called her.

Her willow tree that provided comfort and safety.

It enveloped us and hid us from view, as we enjoyed the cool breeze it provided.

Big Blue, you were there, you were always there.

You saw so much and kept so many of our secrets.

You were there when death came knocking.

First, Vernon alone in a shelter, then Lisa a simple surgery, and Jamie.

Mommy slept for the first time in months the day we took him off life support.

Big Blue, seriously? It wasn't supposed to happen! Life was never the same.

The winds of change blew and Mommy wanted a different life.

The end of an era, didn't know how much I missed you, Big Blue.

Sitting at the counter in Mommy's sun drenched kitchen as she cut fruit and filled plates with crackers and cheese.
I talked.

I didn't know it was her way of listening.

I walk through your rooms one last time. All the familiar smells still there but your walls bare.

I could still hear the sounds of laughter as I move from floor to floor.

Lennette, so eccentric in her style, the bones of her purple hued kitchen still in place.

Quietness fills you now. Fred still remains.

Must be strange all alone with none of the familiar sounds.
"System armed."

I wonder what you were thinking when everyone you knew was finally gone?

They came with scaffolding and tore down your walls.

Big Blue, did you weep?

Big Blue, the big blue bitch as my mother called her, the end of an era.

WALKING ABOVE

Walking above…

Walking in a higher dimension.

Seeing it for the first time, for the last time. Seeing it from a different frame.

A frame, a snapshot, a moment in time.

Time standing still for me to gather my thoughts to put away old things.

Time waited for me. To sing a new tune that caused my heart to swell and join in with heavens crescendo. Lifting my spirit high above, soaring now, leaping now laughing now.

Living above walking in new dimensions.

THE STRUGGLE IS REAL

"And I am convinced that nothing can ever separate us from God's love. Neither death nor life, neither angels nor demons, neither our fears for today nor our worries about tomorrow—not even the powers of hell can separate us from God's love. No power in the sky above or in the earth below—indeed, nothing in all creation will ever be able to separate us from the love of God that is revealed in Christ Jesus our Lord."

—Romans 8:38-39 (NLT)

CUSHITE NATION, ARISE

Arise; this is your finest hour, the dawning of a new day.

Arise and take your place. Fulfill your destiny.

Shake off the sackcloth and ashes. Put on the garment of praise.

How shall they be led? Except ye, Arise, Cushite Nation, Arise.

Remember when God called you and set you above many as Kings and Queens.

Remember when God anointed you and called you Great.

Gird up your loins. Remember not your captivity.

This is your finest hour. This is your time in the kingdom.

Arise, Cushite Nation, Arise!

MISS EDITH

There is wisdom in her. The way she surveyed the room,
sitting proudly in her seat.

I knew that, behind the gentleness in her smile,

there were years of hard-learned lessons.

There is wisdom in her eyes. The knowledge and the stories
that she could drop.

I would love to sit at her feet with my head on her knee as
she speaks her story gently to me.

There's wisdom in her face. Not in the lines that crease it,

but in the regal way she walks into the room.

The past and the present came with her. I saw the future in
her too.

There's wisdom in her hands. The way she gracefully folds
them in her lap.

I wonder how many babies those hands have gently caressed,

how many braids have been platted with those
graceful hands.

I saw the past, the present, and the future in her too.

There is wisdom in her.

UNTITLED

I cried today, but not tears of joy like some say.

But tears that came from a place that I didn't know existed within in me.

Hot tears. Wrenching tears.

Tears that welled up from my past like a stream that had been damned.

Tears that brought up the loneliness and all the misunderstanding.

I cried today like it was the first time and like it would be my last time.

And so I cried today wondering what had caused this.

Wondering what had broken open the well of my soul.

NANA'S HANDS

Nana's hands, oval nails like my mother's, like mine.

Hands that have caressed generations of our naked behinds.

Those hands gently wiped our tears and pressed our heads into

her bosom as she rocked us to sleep.

Hands that created patterns from newspaper, crocheted hats, and painted portraits.

Hands that told us stories about Devil's Wood Yard and Grandma Betty.

Hands that fed rich white women too feeble to know

she was there so she could send her girls to school.

Nana's hands that smelled like rose water.

Flour covered hands that kneaded bread as she talked us through the art of it all.

Hands that dug into the earth and planted gardens that brought forth

their secrets throughout the year.

Nana's hands with the gold wedding band that let me know

she loved and had been loved.

My Nana's hands.

Hands that have aged and grown weak that grasp mine

to steady herself.

Hands that have wisdom not yet shared.

My Nana's hands,

Hands that smelled like rose water.

TRINIDAD

The rhythmic sound of a nation, black faces, red faces, white faces. A melting pot.

The center of the earth. The gathering place for many.

The rhythmic sound of a nation, dialects, slang, secretly coded messages

that make up the fabric of the people.

The sound of the music. The beat, the pounding of the drums.

The piercing sound of the horns almost becomes deafening.

The rhythmic sound of a nation. The sound of the horns, the chatter, clang, bang, bang!

Such noise from the disquiet in the soul of the fabric of a nation.

The hustle, the bustle, smells of spices, urine, and people sleeping in the streets.

The scream of a nation.

The sudden quiet that overcomes the rhythmic sound of a nation.

Another day passed, another day experienced.

Tomorrow comes again. The rhythm continues. The rhythm continues, the rhythm continues.

ONYX

A stone dug up from deep within the earth.

Your colors variable, but your core hardened by time.

Once the stone of kings and queens, you lined their dinner tables with your unique beauty.

Engraved in you were the names of the twelve tribes.

You sat upon the shoulders of the high priest.

You presented the people before their God.

The fifth wall of the great city of heaven is carved out of you.

Your darkness stands in contrast to the beryl and the jacinth and the amethyst.

You glisten proudly as you reflect your uniqueness from the streets of gold.

A stone dug from deep within the earth.

Your colors variable, but your core hardened by time.

Your uncommon beauty long misunderstood.

Since ancient times you have been artificially reproduced,

passed off as the real thing.

Who and what are you now, Onyx?

A stone dug up from deep within the earth.

Your colors variable, unique, but your core hardened by time.

WHITE HORSE

I tried if for the first time. Sort of embarrassed that I was the only one who hadn't done it before.

The feeling was exhilarating, like nothing I'd ever known.

The explosion in my mind, I soared to places in my being that I didn't know existed.

Whoa!

I came down with a nod. Why am I so sleepy? What happened to that exhilarating feeling?

I road that horse until I was sick the next morning.

Burning on the inside, but scratching on the outside. My bowels let loose. What the hell!

Where is my horse? I need to ride until my mind explodes.

I need to ride like an equestrian in a steeplechase.

Oh God, where is my horse?

I'm sweating, nose running. I need my horse, damn it. I gotta jones, but it ain't no love.

I need my horse. Headed to the barn to saddle her up so I can ride.

Ride until I chase this jones away. Ride until I'm free.

Tried it for the first time today. Nobody told me we would be inseparable.

THE HOOD DOES WHAT THE HOOD DOES

A voice cries!

The sound of shattering glass

Flames light the night and set aglow the faces of the people.

A fist raised in the air.

The scent of anger hangs like a wet blanket drenching everyone in its wake.

They push forward, shoulder-to-shoulder.

A chant is heard trickling through the crowd,

"No justice, no peace."

It grows louder, a feverish pitch, it swells and becomes louder and louder and louder.

The sound of it like cymbals reverberates through the night.

Somewhere, a mother cuddles her son, a father stands watch.

An old church mother cries, "Lawd, we need you, Jesus. Come by here."

A nation transfixed.

Today, we're one people.

The guns have been put away, no news today of another prince taken.

What about tomorrow?

Will we go back to feigned laughter and standing on the corners, swaying to whatever?

What about tomorrow?

Will we lift our heads and teach our children to never forget?

Will we go back to low riders pumping profanity-laced music and pants around the hips,

video vixens and knock off Gucci's?

A voice cries

Anger on slow burn

Streets are quiet now, folks lurking in the shadows.

The Hood Does, What the Hood Does.

FREEDOM COME

How many black bodies done swung from them trees?

Rustling through the night crouching deep longing for freedom.

Strange fruit swaying in the morning breeze, freedom come one way or other.

Somewhere off in the distance the sound of wailing and singing. Oh my lord, lord, lord.

They cry for freedom.

Hounds calling, fire burning everything in its wake. Smoke rising, bodies swaying,

Freedom come one way or another.

The sun coming up over the horizon. Running now, heading toward the clearing,

We stop in our tracks, putting our fingers to our lips motioning to keep quiet.

A woman screams as they tie the rope around his neck.

Trapped between here and there, not sure what to do.

We crouch deep, longing for freedom.

How many bodies done swung from them trees?

YOUR BLACK AIN'T LIKE MINE

Your black ain't like mine.

The color of my skin is dark chocolate

With a dip of honey to take the bitterness away

Your black ain't like mine.

Kinky coily hair like a lions mane, some say I need to put a hot comb to it

But I was born this way.

Almond shaped eyes that have seen things far beyond my years.

Standing in the mirror examining this face, this body, I see my mother and my grandmother.

They ain't black like me.

Got broad hips made for bearing children

Thick sturdy legs, men whistle when I walk by.

Your black ain't like mine.

Milk, like sugar-sweet and sticky, almost translucent

See your black ain't like mine.

DAUGHTERS OF ZION

Shape and molded by the hands of a master sculptor
God's grand finale.
Skin the color of mahogany, honey and ginger
Back straight, head held high
Arrayed in the finest Egyptian linen.
The mother of all creation
Who did hinder you?
Who spoke Un-speakable things in you spirit and caused you to believe a lie?
Who touched you in Un-touchable places?
You were once filled with destiny and purpose
Now fear and shame.
Daughters of Zion...
Who did hinder you?

WONDERFUL ME!

"I will praise thee; for I am fearfully and wonderfully made: marvelous are thy works; and that my soul knoweth right well."

—Psalm 139:14 (KJV)

VARIATIONS

Day by Day

Night by Night

Hour by Hour

Changing your ways

From man to woman

Boy to Girl

In a state of constant transformation

Black to White

Rich to Poor

From this to that

That to this

Nobody really knows who you are.

Do you?

Chasing a dream that was never meant to be

Always being something or somebody,

Someone else wanted you to be

Never really being you

Whoever that may be

Always in a state of transformation

Forever changing from this to that, that to this

Never knowing who or what you'll be from one minute to the next

On the biggest ego trip

For who? You?
Who are you?
Nobody really knows.
Do you?

MOMMY

I never thought I looked like you
People always said I did.
Today, I see my face in yours and
For the first time, I know who I am.
I see legacy in your face,
I see my future in your face,
I see the mother you are,
I see the woman you are,
I see your hopes and your dreams,
I've felt your struggle and your fears.
I prayed for you,
Asking God, Please, help her hold on.
I wanted nothing more than to make you happy,
To see you smile.
Today, I see my face in yours.
For the first time, I know who I am.
I know who I am.

(For my mother)

CREATED ANEW

"For we are God's masterpiece. He has created us anew in Christ Jesus, so we can do the good things he planned for us long ago."
—Ephesians 2:10 (NLT)

Not what I used to be, but not what I'm going to be.

Created anew.

No longer dwelling on the should'a, could'a, would'a

Should have said but didn't.

Felt hurt, but pretended that I didn't.

Created anew.

Destiny walking in my life, bringing me to the place predestined for me,

Reaching forward, striding higher,

Created anew.

Not who and what I used to be, but pressing forward to who I shall be,

Created anew.

For His purpose,

My thoughts are not the same, my mindset has changed.

Destiny walking in my life.

Not who and what I used to be,

Pressing forward to who I shall be,

Created anew!

IN MY FATHER'S HOUSE

In my father's house, I learned that Black is beautiful
from my big hips and kinky hair...

I FEEL HERE

I feel here
No longer invisible
My voice has a sound that I never heard before
Silence is no longer part of my persona
I feel here
Present, now, at this moment
This place in time
Time that I never experienced
I feel here
No longer invisible
I am larger than life
I feel here
My voice has a sound that I never heard before
Silence is no longer part of my persona
I feel here!

DO YOU SEE ME?

In all of my splendor. The glory that is me. Light shining from the inside out.

Do you see me?

Twirling with my arms out stretched.

Drinking in the warmth of the sun as blades of grass gently caress my ankles.

No longer bound.

I have been transformed into the glorious woman you see before you.

I've come full circle, freed from my past.

I scream with joy. The sound echoing in my ear.

Do you see me?

UNIQUE

I am a unique being.
Made in the image of an almighty God
Not a carbon copy of another
Unique in my being
Unique in my flow
Created to be just me
Free to be uniquely me
Gifted in my speech
Spirited in my step
I am a unique being.
Creative in the way I do what I do
Created to be just me
Not a carbon copy
No longer trying to fit in and conform
I am a unique being.
Created in the image of the Master
Uniquely Me!
Unable to identify me, place labels on me
Free to be, free to embrace
Uniquely me, wonderful me
Ah, I am a unique being.
Created by the almighty
Do you hear the sound of my name?

Kind and noble, that's me, uniquely me
Named by, called by the Master
A uniquely created being
Shaped by they master
Not a carbon copy

WONDERFUL ME

who am i that i should think
that i should be
or even smile
what gives me the right
to dance and twirl to dip my hip
to feel the sensuous beat
to see the sunlight skip across the dawn
who am i that i should think
that i should be
or even smile
what gives me the right
to sing and crescendo
and sound like crystal
who am i that i should think
that i should be
or even smile
what gives me the right
to lift my eyes
and spread my arms to embrace myself
who am i... i am just me
wonderful me, flawed though i may be
i have the right to be just me
Selah!

BREATHE AGAIN!

Hmm, So I spoke to my God
I rose from the ashes
Not from the place you thought I should have been
Each of us is created for a purpose
Even somebody like me
God breathed and told me to rise
So out of the ashes I rose
No longer looking back at the burning cinders that
once was my life
No longer smelling like the smoke that burnt away
who I was
So, I spoke to my God
And
HE told me to rise
Not from the place you thought I should
I rose as the Authentic Me!

BIBLIOGRAPHY

Pentimenti Women's Writers Group. *Writings Ahhh! the Love* (n.p., 2014)

ABOUT THE AUTHOR

Heidi Lewis is an author, businesswoman, minister, and activist. After earning her bachelor of science in management from Boston University, she earned her master of business administration in organizational leadership. The founder of On Broken Pieces, a para-church ministry that provides holistic support to women, she is an advocate for women's rights, bringing awareness to domestic violence and sexual assault. She is the host and producer of the In My Father's House Radio Broadcast and is a member of the Pentimenti Women's Writer Group.

Lewis currently resides in Boston. She is an NFL football enthusiast and, in her free time, she enjoys playing fantasy football.

CREATING DISTINCTIVE BOOKS
WITH INTENTIONAL RESULTS

We're a collaborative group of creative masterminds with a mission to produce high-quality books to position you for monumental success in the marketplace.

Our professional team of writers, editors, designers, and marketing strategists work closely together to ensure that every detail of your book is a clear representation of the message in your writing.

Want to know more?
Write to us at info@publishyourgift.com
or call (888) 949-6228

Discover great books, exclusive offers, and more at
www.PublishYourGift.com

Connect with us on social media

@publishyourgift

www.ingramcontent.com/pod-product-compliance
Lightning Source LLC
Chambersburg PA
CBHW071537080526
44588CB00011B/1700